Polar Exploration Adventures

by Barbara Saffer

Consultant:
Henry H. Brecher
Research Associate (Retired)
Byrd Polar Research Center
Ohio State University

CAPSTONE BOOKS

an imprint of Capstone Press
Mankato, Minnesota

Capstone Books are published by Capstone Press
151 Good Counsel Drive, P.O. Box 669, Mankato, Minnesota 56002
http://www.capstone-press.com

Library of Congress Cataloging-in-Publication Data
Saffer, Barbara.
    Polar exploration adventures/by Barbara Saffer.
    p. cm.—(Dangerous adventures)
    Includes bibliographical references (p. 45) and index.
    Summary: Examines the history of polar exploration and the adventures of some
polar explorers.
    ISBN 0-7368-0572-9
    1. Polar regions—Discovery and exploration—Juvenile literature. [1. Polar
regions—Discovery and exploration. 2. Explorers.] I. Title. II. Series.
    G587 .S33 2001
    919.8—dc21   00-022388

Editorial Credits
Carrie A. Braulick, editor; Heather Kindseth, cover designer and illustrator;
    Linda Clavel, illustrator; Katy Kudela and Jodi Theisen, photo researchers

Photo Credits
Archive Photos, 10, 22, 24, 32, 34
Gordon Wiltsie, 40
Index Stock Imagery, 28
International Stock/C. Bonington, cover
Kjell Sandved/Pictor, 8
Northwind Picture Archives, 13
Paul Thompson/FPG International LLC, 16, 18, 27
TOM STACK & ASSOCIATES, 43
Visuals Unlimited/Jeanette Thomas, 4; McCutcheon, 7

1 2 3 4 5 6 06 05 04 03 02 01

Table of Contents

Chapter 1

Polar Exploration

For centuries, people have been fascinated with the icy regions surrounding the North and South Poles. The North Pole is a point located at the northern end of the Earth's axis. This imaginary line runs through the middle of the Earth. The Earth spins on its axis. The South Pole is a point located at the southern end of the Earth's axis.

Early explorers traveled to the polar areas for various reasons. Many explorers wanted to claim new territory for their countries. Others wanted to learn about new places. The years from about 1890 to 1920 often are called "the heroic age of polar exploration." Many explorers tried to become the first people to reach the North and South Poles during this time period.

Antarctica has many mountains. One of these mountains is Mount Erebus.

The Arctic

The area surrounding the North Pole is called the Arctic. This area lies inside an imaginary line called the Arctic Circle. This line is located 1,625 miles (2,615 kilometers) from the North Pole.

The Arctic Ocean makes up most of the Arctic. Ice covers the Arctic Ocean. The ice sometimes breaks up to form huge plates of ice called floes. A floe's average thickness is 12 feet (3.7 meters).

Wind and water currents often move floes. Floes form narrow channels of water called leads when they drift apart. The floes form tall ice mounds when they crash together.

The Arctic also includes many islands and the northern parts of Asia, Europe, and North America. Snow and ice cover the land most of the year. The Arctic climate is very cold. Arctic temperatures can drop as low as -90 degrees Fahrenheit (-68 degrees Celsius).

The Arctic has long periods of total darkness during winter. It is dark 24 hours a day between September and March at the North Pole.

Ice floes often move apart to form leads.

The Antarctic

The area surrounding the South Pole is called the Antarctic. This area lies inside an imaginary line called the Antarctic Circle. This line is located 1,625 miles (2,615 kilometers) from the South Pole.

The continent of Antarctica makes up most of the Antarctic. This land mass has many mountains and valleys. Antarctica is almost entirely covered with a large sheet of ice. The

Ice in the Antarctic can form a variety of shapes.

ice sheet has many deep cracks called crevasses.
The Pacific, Atlantic, and Indian Oceans
surround Antarctica.

Antarctic weather is cold and harsh.
Temperatures there can drop as low as
-128 degrees Fahrenheit (-89 degrees Celsius).
This is the lowest temperature ever recorded
in the world. Wind speeds can reach as high as
200 miles (322 kilometers) per hour. The
Antarctic has frequent blizzards.

Antarctic winter begins in March and ends in September. At the South Pole, it is dark 24 hours a day from late March to late September.

Locating the Poles

The early explorers tried to plan the best routes to the poles. But maps of the polar areas were incomplete during this time. Explorers relied on their skills. They also followed other explorers' notes from previous expeditions to help them find the poles.

Polar explorers also used an instrument called a sextant. They measured the height of the sun above the horizon with the sextant. They then examined tables that showed the position of the sun. The explorers then were able to tell how far north or south they were.

Some explorers used compasses. These instruments help people find the direction in which they are traveling. Compasses have a magnetic needle. This needle always points toward the North Magnetic Pole. This point is about 900 miles (1,400 kilometers) south of the North Pole.

Chapter 2

Fridtjof Nansen

Norwegian scientist Fridtjof Nansen was one of the best known Arctic explorers. Nansen wanted to perform studies in the Arctic and reach the North Pole.

In 1893, Nansen and his 12 crewmembers left Oslo, Norway. They sailed a ship called the *Fram* to an area of the Arctic Ocean north of Russia.

Nansen allowed the ship to become locked between ice floes. He hoped the *Fram* would drift to the North Pole. As the *Fram* drifted, Nansen and his crew studied the water's temperature and its salt content. They also studied weather conditions. But after two years, the *Fram* was still 410 miles (660 kilometers) from the North Pole.

Fridtjof Nansen organized many important Arctic expeditions.

On March 14, 1895, Nansen and crewmember Hjalmar Johansen left the ship. They decided to travel to the North Pole on foot.

The Journey North

Nansen knew the *Fram* would continue to drift while he and Johansen were gone. He planned to return to Franz Josef Land. This group of islands is about 600 miles (1,000 kilometers) south of the North Pole. Nansen thought that he and Johansen would meet seal hunters there to take them home.

Nansen and Johansen had prepared for their long journey. They took sleds, sled dogs, skis, and sleeping bags. They also brought a tent, guns, food, and other supplies. They brought two kayaks to help them cross leads. These narrow, covered boats hold one person.

Nansen and Johansen traveled north for three weeks. At first, Nansen and Johansen made good progress. The men were able to travel as far as 20 miles (32 kilometers) per day. The explorers then encountered uneven ice surfaces. They had to push the sleds over ice mounds.

Shipbuilders designed the *Fram* for Nansen's voyage.

Nansen and Johansen traveled to within 260 miles (418 kilometers) of the North Pole. This was farther north than anyone had traveled before. But they were unable to travel any farther. Nansen and Johansen were cold and tired. Their food supply was running low. The men decided to travel south toward Franz Josef Land.

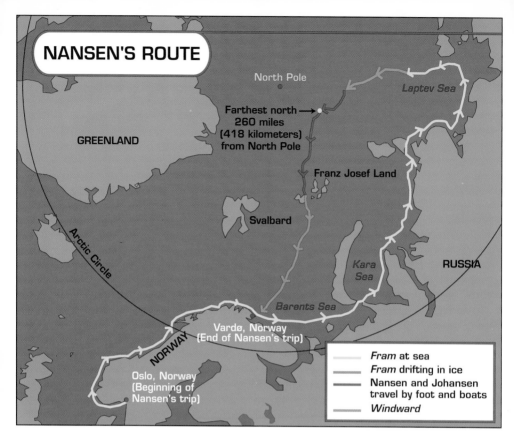

NANSEN'S ROUTE

North Pole

Laptev Sea

Farthest north →
260 miles
(418 kilometers)
from North Pole

GREENLAND

Franz Josef Land

Svalbard

Arctic Circle

Kara
Sea

RUSSIA

Barents Sea

NORWAY

Vardø, Norway
(End of Nansen's trip)

Oslo, Norway
(Beginning of
Nansen's trip)

Fram at sea
Fram drifting in ice
Nansen and Johansen
travel by foot and boats
Windward

The Struggle South

The seasons changed during the explorers'
journey south. The warmer summer weather
caused leads to form. The ice became slushy and
slowed Nansen and Johansen's progress. They
sometimes traveled only 1 mile (1.6 kilometers)
per day.

Nansen and Johansen also began to run out of
supplies for themselves and their dogs. They
killed the weaker dogs to feed to stronger ones.

Nansen and Johansen also sometimes ate the dog meat.

On July 23, 1895, Nansen and Johansen spotted Franz Josef Land. They traveled toward the islands through rain and high winds. One day, a polar bear attacked Johansen. Nansen shot the bear before it killed his companion.

On August 10, 1895, the explorers reached Franz Josef Land. The men then spent the winter on one of the islands.

The Journey Ends

On May 19, 1896, Nansen and Johansen continued their journey. All of their dogs had died. The men pulled the sleds themselves.

On June 17, 1896, Nansen met Sir Frederick Jackson. Jackson was leading a British Arctic expedition. Jackson invited the two explorers to stay at his camp.

A British ship named *Windward* took Nansen and Johansen home. On August 13, 1896, Nansen and Johansen arrived in Vardø, Norway. The two explorers proved that people could survive for long periods of time in the Arctic.

Chapter 3

Robert Peary

Robert Peary was an officer in the United States Navy. He led many expeditions to the Arctic during the late 1800s and early 1900s. African American adventurer Matthew Henson often went with Peary on his expeditions.

Peary tried to reach the North Pole several times. He led one expedition from 1898 to 1902. But Peary's feet became frostbitten. This condition occurs when cold temperatures freeze skin. He ended the journey and returned home. Eight of his toes later had to be cut off due to frostbite.

In 1905, Peary tried to reach the North Pole again. Peary and his crew traveled within 200 miles (322 kilometers) of the pole. They were farther north than anyone had ever been.

In 1909, Peary received credit for being the first person to reach the North Pole.

But Peary's supplies began to run low. He decided to return home again.

A Successful Journey

In 1908, Peary tried once again to reach the North Pole. He and his crew left New York on a ship called the *Roosevelt*. Several Inuits joined Peary on his expedition. For thousands of years, these native people have lived in the Arctic. They often helped Peary during his expeditions.

The *Roosevelt* landed on Ellesmere Island. This island is located off Greenland's northern coast. Peary then sent small teams of men called advance parties along the route to the North Pole. The teams stored supplies and food in storage areas called depots.

On March 1, 1909, the advance parties completed their work. Peary then divided 26 of his men into teams. Each team had dogs and sleds. Most of these teams were supply teams. These teams stored supplies farther north than the advance parties' locations. The supply teams' sleds were heavy. These teams could travel only 10 miles (16 kilometers) per day.

In 1908, Peary and his crew traveled from New York to Ellesmere Island on the *Roosevelt*.

All the supply teams turned back before the pole. The last supply team turned back on April 1, 1909. Peary was then 153 miles (246 kilometers) from the pole.

Peary, Henson, and four Inuits named Ootah, Ooqueah, Egingwah, and Seegloo continued toward the North Pole. They traveled between 25 and 30 miles (40 and 48 kilometers) per day.

On April 6, 1909, Peary's crew reached the North Pole. Peary planted the U.S. flag in the snow. Peary and the other men then traveled back to Ellesmere Island. The crew used the stored supplies on their way back. They arrived 17 days later.

Shocking News

At Ellesmere Island, Peary boarded the *Roosevelt* and sailed to Greenland. He then received shocking news. He heard that American explorer Frederick Cook had beat him to the North Pole. Cook announced that he had reached the North Pole about a year before Peary. Peary did not believe Cook's story and called Cook a liar. But people believed Cook. They gave him awards and honors.

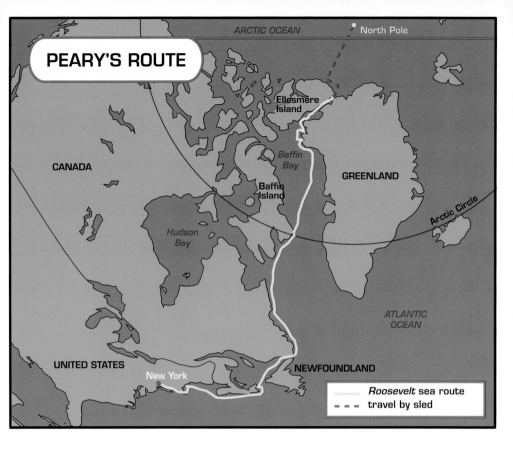

PEARY'S ROUTE

ARCTIC OCEAN · North Pole

Ellesmere Island

Baffin Bay

CANADA

GREENLAND

Baffin Island

Arctic Circle

Hudson Bay

ATLANTIC OCEAN

UNITED STATES

New York

NEWFOUNDLAND

_____ *Roosevelt* sea route
- - - travel by sled

The National Geographic Society studied Peary's and Cook's notes. This organization keeps records of expeditions. On December 15, 1909, the society announced that Peary had reached the North Pole and Cook had not. Today, some polar historians believe that Peary did not reach the North Pole either. They believe his measurements were incorrect. But Peary still is honored for this accomplishment.

Chapter 4

Journeys to the South Pole

Beginning in ancient times, people believed that a continent existed at the bottom of the world. Early explorers tried to find this continent. In 1773, British explorer Captain James Cook became the first person to sail south of the Antarctic Circle.

Different claims exist for who first saw Antarctica's mainland. But in 1820 three explorers received credit for finding the mainland. They were Russian Fabian von Bellingshausen, British explorer Edward Bransfield, and American Nathaniel Palmer. In 1840, American Charles Wilkes sailed along Antarctica's coast.

Roald Amundsen continued polar expeditions until his death in 1928.

A Race for the South Pole

British naval officer Robert Scott wanted to be the first person to reach the South Pole. From 1901 to 1904, he led an expedition to Antarctica. Scott tried and failed to reach the pole during this expedition. In 1910, Scott organized a second expedition to the Antarctic. On June 1, Scott and his crew left England on the ship *Terra Nova*.

Scott thought that he was the only explorer going to the South Pole. But he received a telegram from Norwegian Roald Amundsen when the *Terra Nova* stopped in Australia. The telegram said Amundsen also was traveling to the South Pole. Scott was surprised to learn that he would be in a race to reach the pole.

In January 1911, the *Terra Nova* arrived in Antarctica. Scott and his crew set up a hut called a base camp. The crew stayed in this building until Antarctic spring. The crew could travel more safely in the warmer spring temperatures.

In 1910, Robert Scott planned his second South Pole expedition.

In November 1911, Scott's team left for the South Pole. The support parties went first. These teams stored supplies along the route to the South Pole.

A Difficult Journey

Scott encountered problems with his travel methods during his journey. Scott used few sled dogs. Instead, Scott used ponies and motorized sleds to haul supplies. But the sleds often broke down. The ponies became sick. The crew then had to pull the sleds. This painful and tiring practice is called man-hauling. Scott's crew walked for 9 to 10 hours each day. But they were able to travel only 10 to 13 miles (16 to 21 kilometers) per day.

Scott's food and supplies were unsuitable for his long journey. Scott brought wool clothing instead of fur clothing. Wool does not dry as fast as fur. The explorers often became cold when their clothing became wet. Scott and his men also ate more canned food than fresh food. Canned food lacks vitamin C. This vitamin helps prevent a deadly disease called scurvy.

Scott encountered several other problems during his journey. The crew traveled through

Scott hoped motorized sleds would help him on his polar journey. But these sleds were of little use to him.

many blizzards. Their food and supplies ran low. The men became cold, tired, hungry, and thirsty.

Scott Reaches the Pole

On January 4, 1912, Scott's last supply team turned back. Scott and four others continued the journey. These explorers were Henry Bowers, Edgar Evans, Lawrence Oates, and Edward Wilson. They were about 170 miles (275 kilometers) from the South Pole.

Amundsen reached the South Pole before Scott on December 14, 1911.

On January 16, 1912, Scott's crew saw one of Roald Amundsen's flags planted at the South Pole. The crewmembers felt disappointed. They were not the first people to reach the South Pole. Scott's crew reached the pole on January 17, 1912. The date was 34 days after Amundsen reached the pole.

The Last Journey

Scott and his crew then began the 800-mile (1,287-kilometer) return journey. Temperatures dropped as winter approached. The men were cold and almost starving. Evans and Oates became weak and died.

On March 21, 1912, Scott, Bowers, and Wilson put up their tent for the last time. A blizzard struck and forced them to remain in the tent. The men were freezing and had no food left. The three men wrote farewell notes to their families and friends.

Eight months later, a search party found the bodies of Scott, Bowers, and Wilson. Scott's expedition ended in tragedy. But Scott and his crew still are recognized for their accomplishment.

Roald Amundsen

Norwegian explorer Roald Amundsen wanted to be the first person to reach the North Pole. But Robert Peary reached it first. Amundsen then decided to go to the South Pole.

Amundsen carefully planned his expedition. He learned to drive dogsleds. He brought plenty of fresh food to prevent scurvy. Amundsen also brought fur clothing for his crew. This clothing kept the men warm and dry.

The Expedition

On June 7, 1910, Amundsen and his crew left Norway on the *Fram*. This was the same ship that Nansen had used during his Arctic journey. The *Fram* reached Antarctica on January 14, 1911. Amundsen and his crew then stored supplies along the route. They set up a base camp called Framheim. Like Scott, Amundsen's crew waited until spring to begin their trip to the pole.

On October 20, 1911, Amundsen continued his journey to the South Pole. Four crewmembers named Olav Bjaaland, Sverre Hassel, Helmer Hanssen, and Oscar Wisting went with him.

The explorers made good progress. The men skied while the dogs pulled the sleds. During most days, they traveled for about 5 hours. They covered 15 to 20 miles (24 to 32 kilometers) each day.

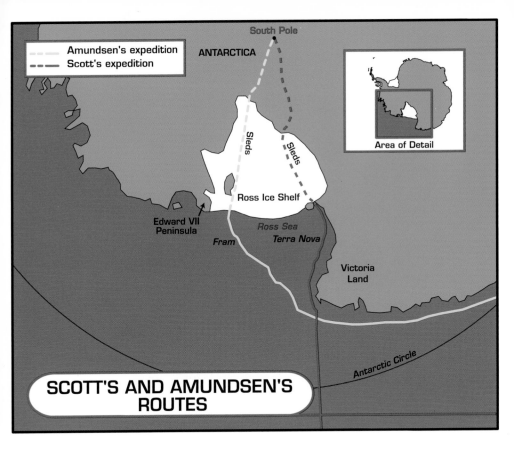

SCOTT'S AND AMUNDSEN'S ROUTES

Amundsen and his crew encountered some difficulties during their journey. They endured many blizzards. The crew also had trouble crossing a large region of broken ice called the Devil's Glacier. But they overcame these problems. On December 14, 1911, they became the first people to reach the South Pole.

Chapter 5

Ernest Shackleton

British explorer Ernest Shackleton made several voyages to the Antarctic. During his Antarctic expedition between 1907 and 1909, he tried to become the first person to reach the South Pole. He came within 112 miles (180 kilometers) of the pole before turning back. This was farther south than anyone had ever traveled before.

Shackleton thought of a new challenge after other explorers reached the South Pole. He planned to cross Antarctica. He hoped to walk from one coast of the continent to the other. This distance is about 1,800 miles (3,000 kilometers).

On August 8, 1914, Shackleton left England on the ship *Endurance*. The ship sailed on the Atlantic Ocean toward Antarctica. Shackleton's

Ernest Shackleton's leadership skills during the *Endurance* expedition made him famous.

Shackleton and his crew stayed at Ocean Camp for about two months.

crew included 27 men. On January 19, 1915, the *Endurance* became trapped in ice less than 100 miles (160 kilometers) from Antarctica. The ship remained locked in the ice for months.

Abandon Ship

In October, the ice began to crush the *Endurance*. Shackleton ordered the crew to carry lifeboats, equipment, and food to a floe beside the ship. On October 27, 1915, Shackleton and his crew moved to the ice floe.

The crew prepared to stay on the ice floe for as long as possible. They put up tents. The men shot seals and penguins to eat. They called the ice floe "Ocean Camp." The crew stayed at Ocean Camp for two months. The *Endurance* sank while they were on the ice floe.

Patience Camp

In December, the warmer summer temperatures caused Ocean Camp to melt. Shackleton and his crew filled their three lifeboats with supplies. They put the lifeboats on sleds and pulled them across the ice.

On December 29, the crew reached another ice floe. They set up a new camp called "Patience Camp." The hungry, cold men stayed at this camp for more than three months.

Elephant Island

By April 8, 1916, most of the ice floes had melted and many leads had formed. Shackleton and his men launched the lifeboats. The men headed for Elephant Island. This small island is off the northern tip of the Antarctic Peninsula. This peninsula is a narrow strip of Antarctica's land that extends into the Atlantic Ocean. Elephant Island was about 100 miles (160 kilometers) away from Patience Camp.

Shackleton's crew reached Elephant Island on April 14, 1916. But people who hunted for whales seldom came to the island. The crew feared that no one would rescue them.

South Georgia Island
On April 24, Shackleton and five men left Elephant Island in the largest lifeboat named *James Caird*. They wanted to reach South Georgia Island. This island was about 800 miles (1,300 kilometers) away. The crew hoped to find people to help them at the island's whaling stations. People who hunted whales lived at these stations.

After 17 days, Shackleton's crew landed on South Georgia Island. But the whaling stations were on the other side of the island.

On May 19, Shackleton and two other crewmembers traveled another 29 miles (47 kilometers) to reach the stations. They traveled over a mountain range. The team climbed mountains that were about 3,000 feet (1,000 meters) high.

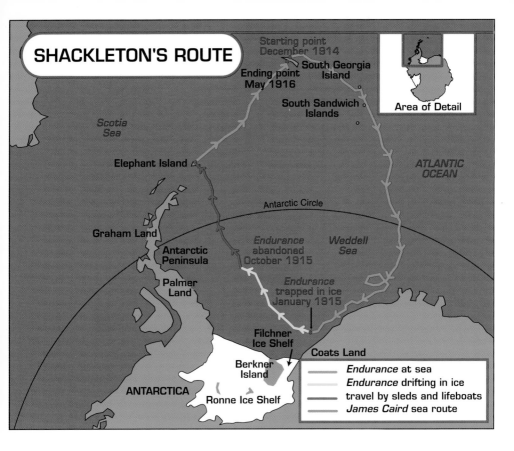

SHACKLETON'S ROUTE

Starting point
December 1914

South Georgia
Island

Ending point
May 1916

South Sandwich
Islands

Area of Detail

Scotia
Sea

Elephant Island

ATLANTIC
OCEAN

Antarctic Circle

Graham Land

Antarctic
Peninsula

Endurance
abandoned
October 1915

*Weddell
Sea*

Palmer
Land

Endurance
trapped in ice
January 1915

Filchner
Ice Shelf

Coats Land

Berkner
Island

ANTARCTICA

Ronne Ice Shelf

Endurance at sea
Endurance drifting in ice
travel by sleds and lifeboats
James Caird sea route

The Rescue

On May 20, the men reached the whaling
stations. The whaling crews welcomed the men.
The next day, a whaling ship rescued the three
crewmembers who were left on the other side
of South Georgia Island.

Shackleton also arranged for a ship to save
the men on Elephant Island. On August 30, 1916,
Shackleton rescued these men. All of Shackleton's
crew returned home safely.

TIMELINE

ARCTIC

1607
British explorer Henry Hudson travels within 600 miles (966 kilometers) of the North Pole.

1827
British explorer William Parry travels within 500 miles (805 kilometers) of the North Pole.

1831
British explorer James Ross discovers the North Magnetic Pole.

1895
Norwegian explorer Fridtjof Nansen travels within 260 miles (418 kilometers) of the North Pole.

1600s   **1800s**

ANTARCTIC

1773
British explorer James Cook crosses the Antarctic Circle.

1820
Russian explorer Fabian von Bellingshausen, British explorer Edward Bransfield, and American explorer Nathaniel Palmer receive credit for finding Antarctica's mainland.

1840
American explorer Charles Wilkes sails along Antarctica's coast.

1841
James Ross discovers the Ross Sea. This sea borders Antarctica.

1895
Norwegian explorer Leonard Kristensen and his crew make first confirmed landing on Antarctica's mainland.

1897
Belgian explorer Adrien de Gerlache leads an Antarctic expedition. His ship becomes trapped in ice. The crew becomes the first people to spend a winter in Antarctica.

1899
Norwegian explorer Carsten Borchgrevink leads the first planned winter expedition in Antarctica.

1903–1906
Norwegian explorer Roald Amundsen and his crew become the first people to sail through a route called the "Northwest Passage." This route is between the Atlantic and Pacific Oceans above Canada.

1909
American explorer Robert Peary receives credit for becoming the first person to reach the North Pole.

1978
Japanese explorer Naomi Uemura becomes the first person to travel to the North Pole alone.

1986
American explorer Ann Bancroft becomes the first woman to travel to the North Pole.

1991
Russian ships begin taking tourists to the North Pole.

1900s

1901–1904
British explorer Robert Scott leads an expedition on Antarctica's mainland.

1911
Roald Amundsen becomes the first person to reach the South Pole.

1914–1916
Ernest Shackleton leads *Endurance* expedition in Weddell Sea.

1990
American explorer Will Steger and his crew complete their journey across Antarctica.

1907–1909
British explorer Ernest Shackleton travels within 112 miles (180 kilometers) of the South Pole.

1912
British explorer Robert Scott reaches the South Pole.

1929
American pilot Richard Byrd and three crewmembers become first people to fly over the South Pole in an airplane.

1994
Norwegian explorer Liv Arnesen becomes first woman to ski to the South Pole alone.

Chapter 6

Modern Polar Exploration

Today, many explorers still travel to the Arctic and the Antarctic. Some of these explorers want to learn about the polar regions. They study the animals that live there. They also may study the water and ice in the regions.

Will Steger

American Will Steger is a modern polar explorer. He reached the North Pole in 1986. He then decided to cross the Arctic and Antarctica. He wanted to study the regions while he traveled.

On July 25, 1989, Steger and five other men began their journey across Antarctica on the Antarctic Peninsula. The men skied behind

Will Steger led an expedition across the Arctic and Antarctica.

dogsleds loaded with supplies. The temperatures were very cold. Frequent blizzards occurred. These blizzards sometimes forced the explorers to stay in their tents for days. Steger and his team studied pollution, ice, and the weather during their journey. On March 3, 1990, the crew completed its journey across Antarctica.

In 1995, Steger led an expedition across the Arctic. He wanted to study the Arctic Ocean. He also wanted to learn about fish and other animals that live in the region.

On March 9, 1995, Steger's team began to cross the frozen Arctic Ocean from northern Canada. They often traveled through heavy snow. Temperatures usually were about -20 degrees Fahrenheit (-29 degrees Celsius). Steger and his team completed their journey across the Arctic on July 3, 1995.

Scientists at the Polar Regions

Today, many scientists perform studies in the polar regions. Research stations exist in Antarctica and on the Arctic land areas.

Many countries have research stations in Antarctica.

Scientists from 18 countries operate Antarctica's research stations. The United States currently operates three of these stations. Many national government and university organizations operate research stations in the Arctic.

The polar regions continue to fascinate people. Explorers and scientists will continue to visit these icy regions to learn more about them.

Words to Know

axis (AK-siss)—an imaginary line that runs through the middle of the Earth; the Earth spins on its axis.

compass (KUHM-puhss)—an instrument people use to find the direction in which they are traveling; compasses have a needle that points north.

crevasse (kri-VAHSS)—a deep crack in an ice sheet

floe (FLOH)—a large chunk of floating sea ice

frostbite (FRAWST-bite)—a condition that occurs when cold temperatures freeze skin

kayak (KYE-ak)—a covered, narrow boat that holds one person

lead (LEED)—a narrow path of water that forms when ice floes move apart

scurvy (SKUR-vee)—a deadly disease caused by lack of vitamin C; scurvy produces swollen limbs, bleeding gums, and weakness.

To Learn More

Bramwell, Martyn. *Polar Exploration: Journeys to the Arctic and the Antarctic.* DK Discoveries. New York: D K Publishing, 1998.

Curlee, Lynn. *Into the Ice: The Story of Arctic Exploration.* Boston: Houghton Mifflin, 1998.

Green, Jen. *Exploring the Polar Regions.* Voyages of Discovery. New York: Peter Bedrick Books, 1997.

McCurdy, Michael. *Trapped by the Ice!: Shackleton's Amazing Antarctic Adventure.* New York: Walker and Company, 1997.

McLoone, Margo. *Women Explorers in Polar Regions.* Capstone Short Biographies. Mankato, Minn.: Capstone Books, 1997.

Useful Addresses

Byrd Polar Research Center
Ohio State University
1090 Carmack Road
Columbus, OH 43210-1002

Institute of Arctic and Alpine
    Research (INSTAAR)
University of Colorado
Campus Box 450
1560 30th Street
Boulder, CO 80309-0450

National Geographic Society
P.O. Box 98199
Washington, DC 20090-8199

Royal Canadian Geographical Society
39 McArthur Avenue
Ottawa, ON K1L 8L7
Canada

Internet Sites

Byrd Polar Research Center
http://www-bprc.mps.ohio-state.edu

Discoverers Web
http://www.win.tue.nl/~engels/discovery/
  index.html

National Geographic.com
http://www.nationalgeographic.com

The New South Polar Times
http://205.174.118.254/nspt/home.htm

Royal Canadian Geographical Society
http://www.rcgs.org

Scott Polar Research Institute's Kids Page
http://www.spri.cam.ac.uk/kids/home.htm

Index